ADVANCE PRAISE FOR *The House of Charlemagne*

"Let this text remind us of politics as empathy, politics as animate, bodily, cardiographic. Let Riel's bristling imagination inhabit us and help us to re-engage the metaphysical dimensions of government, its grounding in what-is, its radical connection to place."—SUE SINCLAIR, author of *Heaven's Thieves*

"Lilburn's masque, rooted in the teachings of Louis Riel and the odyssey of his erstwhile Anglophone disciple, Honoré Jaxon, posits a visionary polity, part Roman Catholic, part Platonist, all deeply rooted in the western prairies. Lilburn steadfastly refuses to separate political life from the life of the imagination. With nods to Julian of Norwich, Marguerite Porete, and Hart Crane, the result is both a script for performance and a document of 'citizenship in a previously unimaginable land'—a visionary charter for a government that has never existed, that Riel insisted must yet exist."
—G.C. WALDREP, author of *Testament*

THE HOUSE OF CHARLEMAGNE

ᎠᏂᏉ
OSKANA POETRY & POETICS

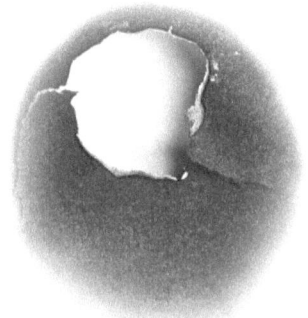

Tim Lilburn

The House of Charlemagne

University of Regina Press

© 2018 Tim Lilburn

All rights reserved. No part of this work covered by the copyrights hereon may be reproduced or used in any form or by any means—graphic, electronic, or mechanical—without the prior written permission of the publisher. Any request for photocopying, recording, taping or placement in information storage and retrieval systems of any sort shall be directed in writing to Access Copyright.

Cover and text design: Duncan Campbell, University of Regina Press

Proofreader: Kristine Douaud

Cover art: "Burnt hole of paper" by Nik Merkulov / iStock.

The text and titling faces are Arno, designed by Robert Slimbach.

Library and Archives Canada Cataloguing in Publication

Lilburn, Tim, 1950–, author
    The House of Charlemagne / Tim Lilburn.

(Oskana poetry & poetics)
Poems.
Issued in print and electronic formats.
ISBN 978-0-88977-530-5 (softcover).—
ISBN 978-0-88977-531-2 (PDF)

I. Title. II. Series: Oskana poetry & poetics

PS8573.I427H68 2018   C811'.54
C2017-907461-X   C2017-907462-8

UNIVERSITY OF REGINA PRESS
University of Regina
Regina, Saskatchewan
Canada S4S 0A2
TELEPHONE: (306) 585-4758
FAX: (306) 585-4699
WEB: www.uofrpress.ca
EMAIL: uofrpress@uregina.ca

We acknowledge the support of the Canada Council for the Arts for our publishing program. We acknowledge the financial support of the Government of Canada. / Nous reconnaissons l'appui financier du gouvernement du Canada. This publication was made possible with support from Creative Saskatchewan's Creative Industries Production Grant Program.

—*an invitation to dialogue and dance*—

produced by New Dance Horizons/Rouge-gorge
September 19, 2015

The work The House of Charlemagne *may not be performed in any version without the consent of Edward Poitras and Robin Poitras.*

for Edward Poitras and Robin Poitras

CONTENTS

13 *Massinahican*
33 The House of Charlemagne

71 Notes and Acknowledgements

MASSINAHICAN

first grass tall as a horsed
man's thigh, plain of bones,
white curls breaking soil, south
to the Souris, north to bear-foot-
printed Riding Mountain
then crossing the Carrot
River, the Wild Cat Hills,
birch, fern, pine duff
and the flats of the Minnichinas Hills, high
plain, Lake Lenore, Quill Lakes,
interior drainage,
swans in loud rumble rising,
eye on a wheel,
toward the Cactus Hills, Dirt Hills, the South
Saskatchewan River, glacial outflow,
fescue, blue grama grass,
buffalo thickening Thunder Creek valley,
marsh heron and snowgeese in April,
ice still in north coulees
and antelope and into the damp, cool
blue smell of the Crowsnest Pass,
river odour, sound of kingfisher and odour
of snows creeping
down wet black rock

I. HONORÉ JAXON

Following his trial in Regina, Honoré Jaxon, Louis Riel's last secretary, was assigned, on August 8, 1885, to the new psychiatric hospital in the Old Stone Fort at Selkirk, Manitoba. Proofs of his insanity, the court heard, were that he was religiously deranged and held that Riel had set fires in his clothes just by brushing by him. There were, Jaxon believed—surprising even himself, his self-boiling self—multiple livable additional worlds. His imagination grew as large as a pulsing peony.

On September 16, he began a four-day fast "on account of the position of Louis Riel," in the words of his doctor, David Young. In a letter to his parents in the days after his fast, he asked them to send ten-pound cases of white clover honey to Poundmaker, Big Bear, Moïse Ouellette and Maxime Lépine, all then in Stony Mountain Penitentiary, and to Louis Riel, now two months from his hanging, in the Northwest Mounted Police stockade in north Regina. This building stood adjacent to land Edgar Dewdney, governor of the Northwestern Territory, owned and hoped would make him even more deliriously rich.

Jaxon reported that he'd accepted Riel as his "director of conscience" before the Battle of Duck Lake on March 29, 1885. If this was so—Riel his spiritual director, friend of his soul—it had political consequences, of course, but what lake of stellar heat did he now float in? What was the cosmos when he looked in?

◆

40. Elles [les essences infinies] l'eussent absorbé entièrement. Elles l'eussent ravi dans les cieux, tout vivant, comme le mouvement sublime des ailes y fait monter le corps volatile de l'aigle, et comme l'air y transporte les objets moins denses et moins forts que la matière de ses gaz invisibles.

—LOUIS RIEL, *Système philosophico-théologique*

The infinite essences would have absorbed the loving man utterly, catching him up into their larger body. A passage of particles that carried political geometries, charted the soul and reseated the badly slanted world. We could be in a text by Proclus or Damascius.

◆

Riel's book *Massinahican* was an attempt to render old Rupert's Land, or at least how it would appear in the new state of Assiniboia, into philosophy, interiority and politics. Grass angle, river system to disposition.

◆

Jaxon saw that his intellectual descent into Riel's imagination had placed him in a no-man's-land, absolutely exposed to wind, wolves and the threat of diabetes out that way. He wrote to his mother: "My joining the Roman Catholic church has cut me off from the assistance of Protestants, while my adoption of Mr. Riel has lost me the countenance of the majority of Roman Catholics." Just what this "adoption" had brought into him was citizenship in a previously unimaginable land, a country beyond the seas, parts of it mentioned, under other names, in three or four old books.

◆

31. Cette rupture peut être plus ou moins complète.

32. Si l'âme fait un acte dont le désordre ne consiste qu'à affaiblir cette harmonie, le péché est véniel. En s'appliquant à faire mieux, elle peut se réhabiliter. Ses efforts pour cela auront assez d'efficacité: c'est-à-dire que par les relations encore assez harmonieuses avec Celui qui Est elle peut naturellement reprendre la force perdue.

—LOUIS RIEL, *Système philosophico-théologique*

◆

The active essences Riel writes about appear to be metaphysical atoms, minute spiritual pellets or ball bearings that produce immateriality as you ingest them or they find ways through your skin. There they sprout storms of themselves. You are struck by an intent lightness, by intimate, slimming perfections that swim up in you.

◆

The young Socrates: *"… for I suppose I have a share of multitude."*

—PLATO, *Parmenides* 129c.

◆

Riel perceives a blowing dust of particles passing through bodies, and they leave behind a spoor of spirit. Once kissed by such clouds, subtly you will be deposited, descending through layers of decades, on a New York City street, the papers of your polis, your real, greater body, mountained around you. You will lean in the direction the stacked archives lean, chin on your cane. Thus the gale in things pushes you.

◆

LITTLE ARM, THEN NORTH, LONG LAKE

Little Arm peels to the south
west, low valley, barn halfway up,
red samphire, dock
along banks, Herefords drift where the lake bends
north. People in Payepot's
generation of tents grew
here, fishing creeks or manhandling sturgeon
from the bigger waters.
Lanigan Creek breeches its weir at the lake's upper
tip
and mallards rise on the freshening.
Along the north-west end

of the water and down
toward the town of Imperial,
dust and slough smell
stretches hundreds of yards into sky,
cranes crying
out of swathed oatfield gray.

◆

That rupture can be more or less complete. If the soul performs an act the disorder of which does not substantially weaken that particular harmony, the sin is venial. In setting her face to the better, she, the soul, can be rehabilitated, reclothed. Her efforts will be sufficient; that is to say, if harmonious relations with That Which Is are re-established, the soul can recover the powers that have been lost.

◆

No one knows the true extent of what was in Riel's *Massinahican*, his title the Cree for "story" or "complete account." What the book holds is what had preoccupied him from 1881 to 1884 at the small school in Montana where he taught: monads, gender, in fact the whole fine machinery of the universe. We do not know when or how most of the text was lost. It may have vanished in the chaos of flight, as he travelled by horse with Gabriel Dumont, Moïse Ouellette, Michel Dumas, and James Isbister seven hundred miles through buffalo country east of the Cypress Hills, along the Missouri Coteau, around the giant sturgeoned waters of Last Mountain Lake, to a cluster of whitewashed cabins on a cliff above the South Saskatchewan River named St. Laurent. The few numbered sections that remain show a philosophical-theological system that resembles an amalgam of Neoplatonism—in its anticipations of human completeness arising from contact with physical objects bristling with metaphysical presence—and Taoism—in the recognition of the ethics-forming power in the mere structure of the world. This is not to say Riel was an Iamblichean Platonist or philosophical Taoist or blender of the two, though his own studies and conversations with the young classicist Jaxon may have taken him into these regions. Mostly he picked up what was in the air or what he heard from Big Bear or read in notes taken by Baptiste Arcand from conversations with the same *mistahi-maskwa*.

◆

Edward Poitras represented Canada at the Venice Biennale in 1995 with an image of the trickster coyote made out of coyote bones assembled in a violent, post-crash, cliffy manner. "We all do coyote," he remarked in an interview.

Jaxon himself had an interest in disarrangement and showed a pitched availability to the undermining in the eruption of the new. His door stood open for the coyote.

◆

THE NEW

Robert Lowell, knocked out by Pius's shout
at Mary's rushing body,
1950, in an ascending aluminum
tube, where dark eyes,
nineteenth-century Force, Little Flower
mystic toffee melt
into each other in heat of stratospheric friction to
something near the smell of ivy
creeping from damp earth; Lowell slumped,
stunned, fighting his breath, in his train car ratcheting through the Alps,
the sting in him as in Jung,
rapt before the declaration
of the Assumption of Mary,
listens as waiters beat gongs
along the aisles for lunch.
Pius sang so recently a night,
alone, absence with gravity, on the eastern camps.
After the destruction of the Temple,
Rabbi Akiba announced the gates
of prayer were closed
but the gates of weeping swung free.
Before Lowell, jetted within the column

of the woman,
whoosh and blade of her rising
jeweled with airlessness' gloss, before him
rivered—heat-marked bull's tongue—meaning.
For Jung, snicking breeches
for trickles by a lake close, the
quaternity shone from the papal bedroom
mouth, and so appeared frayed female
waves, webby revenants
in space and general matter.

◆

Sung in the self's theatre, under low lights, Riel, before an audience composed solely of the self in its several forms: "O Virgin Mary, Tower of Ivory, deign to accept all my writings in good faith, particularly the *Massinahican*. Bless all these writings, if it please you, and if they are acceptable to my God. Deign to obtain of Jesus Christ, if it please Him, that fear and terror be thrown into the heart of Monsigneur Brondel, of Monsigneur Taché, of all the French-Canadian episcopacy, of the whole Roman curia and of the whole English court, by means of the *Massinahican* …."

Riel speaks to the woman he carried inside his coat. Brondel and Taché were the bishops of Helena, Montana and St. Boniface respectively. Riel's political-theological shaping of onto-corrective phenomenology was intentionally incendiary, meant to form, control burn, a church that would lodge above Holy Church, in the formulation of the beguine Marguerite Porete. By this, he would launch a psychagogic politics designed to unfasten the nerves of the British Empire.

He had intended to publish the book on his own and pour fire on the English court and its Canadian spear-carriers, yet he believed the church's grandees were reachable still if they chose to expose their interior selves to complete annihilation.

The Church's own sapiential tradition had walked away from it and discovered rest under cardboard in bending grass near discarded chemical containers, where Riel had found bits and pieces and crocheted them together. But all persons were pulled, he knew, even if they refused to recognize it, even if they believed they opposed it, to the eros of philosophy. He said to his brother Joseph: "Instead of publishing my book, as I told you, I thought it would be good for the Métis nation and for others and that I would give great pleasure to Monsigneur Taché, if I came to Manitoba and said to him, 'Monsigneur, here is what I have written …'."

We know that Riel did not take the *Massinahican* to Manitoba in 1883 and he may not have taken it to Saskatchewan two years later. Perhaps the bulk of it was left behind in the house he and his family shared with another teacher at St. Peter's Mission on the Sun River. There the book could have been burned by inattention as the library at Alexandria had burned. With rains, the document liquified, yet kept for a moment a shape, then one drop attached to another and the whole drained into fissures in the ground.

◆

Along the Sun River, there the book had its own bed of leaves near the sparse water. Inside its wonder glass, at which the book itself ceaselessly stared, the universe is a lake of deathless essences, some active, some holding back, waiting, looking around. Within these essences are monads, concrete yet non-detectable, dark energy, dark matter, force at a distance, hidden from the most reaching nomination, hidden inside the speed of everything. The monads appear in male and female pairs, positive and negative electrical charges. Thus love. Thus shape. The monadic organization determines each instance of what declares that it is.

The male and female monadic pairs, sitting in a tree, Edenic, kissing.

◆

La religion consiste à relier (religare) les essences humaines et les essences divines ensemble.

—LOUIS RIEL, *Système philosophico-théologique*

Let female and male be bound with electrical tape. A confluence of triggered streams.

Let divinity cascade into a vial around which one's skin has grown.

◆

These revelations were shown to a simple, uneducated creature on the eighth of May, 1373. Some time earlier, she had asked three gifts of God.

—JULIAN OF NORWICH, *Revelations of Divine Love*

◆

Riel rubs moonmilk into charcoal at the centre of what will be a cougar's head. The cat forms, ballooning from his eye, birthed on the wall. Juniper wick flame sends light travelling on the stone, mycelium for the myth. And from this eye a world spreads.

Such audacity would naturally mean death in a xenophobic, policedly realist country like ours. He walks nude, Adamic, through the bedroom of Princess Louise, Duchess of Argyll.

◆

Le sexe est dans les monades c'est-à-dire que chaque monade alterne a sa forme mâle et sa forme femelle.

Chaque monade active mâle possède en propre une monade inerte qui est femelle.

Et chaque monade active femelle possède en propre une monade inerte qui est mâle.

—LOUIS RIEL, *Système philosophico-théologique*

♦

The female and the male each seed an ear-mote into the other, verdant hearing growing into each as a vine.

♦

Under thy shadow by the piers I waited;
Only in darkness is thy shadow clear.
The City's fiery parcels all undone,
Already snow submerges an iron year …

—HART CRANE, from "To Brooklyn Bridge," *The Bridge*

♦

When I left Eli Zabar the cut-out star on the window
was whirling in the animation of the rich and hungry
hunched over tables for a $30 sandwich and a Diet Coke.

It was raining and the blurred glass of the galleries
was the gold leaf of Carrig Rhone frames—
Childe Hassam's dabs of Connecticut trees

the diaphanous blue on the fleshy rocks,
the melting opal of the shoals.
In the Whitney the rain trailed down my face;

and I found myself in a quiet corner staring
at the pink face of Marilyn Monroe.
I could still smell the smoldering high-tech plastic

as it burned the air. The whiteness of her teeth,
in the almost aahh of her mouth and the half-drugged eyes
under lids of teal shadow, the air kept singeing my nose.

—PETER BALAKIAN, from "Warhol/Madison Ave./9-11," *Ziggurat*

◆

Jaxon turned up in New York after labour-organizing in Chicago. He lived in a small fort tacked together from empty ammunition boxes along the Bronx River, then had a room next to the furnace in an apartment building, a furnace to which he fed coal. Then he was thrown out, spooked, buffalohunter-hatted, and the national library, intellectual bullion stash of the Second Provisional Government of Assiniboia formed at Batoche, was stacked in the street around him, waiting for a truck to haul it to the dump. Took up nearly a complete block. Jaxon's look in the one photo we have of that moment is a tiny spider climbing around the camera's lens. He can't weigh more than 120 pounds, and he's tilted into the spin of the Earth.

◆

William Henry Jackson, eldest son of a shopkeeper in Prince Albert, District of Lorne, North-West Territories, seemed someone unlikely to marry a year-old deer or place a finger into the boil of elements and taste. A bright young man, he was the first from the North-West wilderness, Great Lone Land, to pursue university studies, absorbing classics at the University of Toronto, where I imagine he contemplated writing an honour's thesis on block-long male and female phoenixes dwelling at the suppressed center of Book IV of the *Aeneid*, "The Passion of the Queen." His family went west from Wingham, Ontario, in 1881, and William Henry followed a couple of years later, believing he was a glorious streaming bird in transit, joining his father who had set up a general store in Prince Albert and a brother who'd opened a pharmacy. Henry took up a land grant and started farming in the district in 1883.

The decade from 1871 to 1881 had been good for farming in the western territories, with rains coming at helpful times and the grain consistently ripening before freezing, lucky since frost-hardy wheat varieties hadn't then been developed. But in the ten years following this promising beginning, droughts and early frosts reduced or completely destroyed yields, while grain buyers took any opportunity to drive down the price of wheat; a frozen crop in a small part of Manitoba in 1883 meant severely cut payments to all farmers everywhere. Meanwhile rising equipment costs, isolation, difficulties in getting one's crop to market, and the federal government's favouritism toward railways and milling companies wore down many farmers, causing a great number of them to abandon homesteads, while the same forces radicalized those who managed to stay on the land.

Meetings in settlements in southern Manitoba gave birth to the Manitoba and North-West Farmers' Union, which drew up a farmers' bill of rights modeled on a similar document produced by Riel's first Provisional Government in 1869–70. A Settlers' Union, formed in the town of Qu'Appelle around the same time, pursued similar ends—land reform and policies favouring residents in the North-West rather than distant corporations, railways, and the federal government. A branch of this union in the District of Lorne sought to league itself with the Métis at St. Laurent, and young Jackson, secretary of the Union, Latin and Greek pollened around his tongue, Plato's *Republic* at his bedside, was sent to inquire into this possible bond. He discovered considerable interest, and at a meeting uniting French and English in the area, Métis and non-Métis, on May 6, 1884, he voted with others to send a delegation into Montana country south of the Missouri River to speak with Louis Riel, for it was he who had negotiated the Manitoba Act that had won all Métis and recently arrived farmers in the area their dignity and their rights. Jackson's listening at this meeting and later ones would soon alter his name and sculpt his life as a river does sandbars.

◆

Phoenixes, one male, one female, nearly filling the narthex, stream, flying, in unison, in church air, touching the ceiling, brushing statues in the Cathedral of St. John the Divine across the street from Columbia University on Manhattan's Upper West Side, and spill construction debris from the collection of saw-offs, roll ends that make up their bodies.

II. THE DANCE

The House of Charlemagne, a dance and opera for chant, was staged September 19, 2015, the last night of the festival "Performing Turtle Island," which had drawn First Nations creators to southern Saskatchewan from across the continent to perform their work through the week-long event. The venue for the dance/masque/opera was the cavernous Riddell Theatre at the University of Regina.

The House was the conception of the Métis artist Edward Poitras, one of Canada's premier visual magi. He acted as the piece's conceiver, set designer, dramaturge and its foremost and governing dreamer. A year before the production, Edward had invited me to write a performable poem based on Jaxon's life, in particular his period with Riel and Honoré's last days. The piece was to have three scenes—Jackson's initial meetings with Riel; their respective imprisonments; and Jaxon on the street in New York, the collected papers of Riel's Second Provisional Government stacked around him. Edward also wanted mention made of the burning of the ancient library at Alexandria and Pope Alexander VI's 1493 decree, *Inter Caetera*, which granted all lands in the Western hemisphere "not held by a Christian prince" to the Spanish crown. He was particularly curious about the roots of Jaxon's commitment to Riel: what had ignited the young man's mind? I was told to write with a troupe of four male dancers in mind. Early in the process of making the show, before I'd done much writing, I'd asked Robin Poitras, Edward's frequent co-creator, how long he'd been thinking about William Henry Jackson/Honoré Jaxon, and she replied she thought it was around forty years.

The piece's subtitle was *A Dance in Three Acts: The Life of William Henry Jackson and His Brief Time with Louis Riel*. The primary dancers were Bill Coleman (the old Honoré), Graham Kotowich (the young Honoré), Eloi Homier, Marcus Merasty, Yvonne Chartrand, Krista Solheim, these joined by Ray Ambrosi and Yawen Luo, all moving under the choreographical direction of Robin Poitras. Jeff Bird, of Cowboy

Junkies renown, supplied the music on synthesizer and flute. He played on the side of the stage, facing the dancers at an oblique angle and seemed often to be improvising the score as the massed dancers surged toward him and receded. I sat at a similar angle on the other side of the stage and sent large sections of the poem skittering into the movement unfolding in front of me. Sound artist Charlie Fox suffused the hall with gathered sounds of geese in flight, wind, gunshots, water streaming around stones.

"Once upon a time in the West," Edward Poitras wrote in the program, "a right hand and a wolf's head etched in history did echo and were heard through the ages, beyond notions of race and time, beyond the veil of words, a song of eternal life in death. Above the hubris of those who would make war. A western with no end, chasing its tail towards the setting sun in twilight's last trace before the night and the light of a new day. From the archives of Honoré Jaxon comes a dance in three acts. In a journey through time and space from Batoche 1885 to New York 1951." The right hand and wolf's head were flag symbols of the Métis nation.

Across the Wide Missouri, Along the Great Divide, Distant Drums, The Battle of Powder River, Warpath, Westward the Women—films released in 1951, their titles displayed on Manhattan theatre marquees.

The House was dedicated to the memory of Roger Ing (1933–2008) and the New Utopia Café on Dewdney Ave. in north-central Regina, a gathering place for artists, nursery for an ocean of ideas, for years.

Rehearsals for *The House of Charlemagne*, which Edward had renamed *The House of Chow Mein* in the days before the performance, took place through early September, things getting patched together as we went along. Female dancers were added. Edward Poitras told the newspaper *Prairie Dog* that the original title echoed a prophecy Riel made about Manitoba in 500 years: "Down the road, he said, Manitoba would be totally French Canadian and would have 40 million souls. Manitoba is an indigenous word meaning 'the great spirits crossing,' and it made me wonder if maybe he was referring to Manitoba in that sense as opposed to thinking of it as a province." The name of this state of mind would be, for a time, the House of Charlemagne. An earlier name had been Assiniboia.

◆

It should be noted that the directions to dancers in the following poem are *not* those used in the actual performance, but merely signposts to help me imagine my way through the pre-performance text.

For the performance, I shredded the poem and spoke the lines it seemed to me the movement of the dancers required.

◆

Edward Poitras made a journey to New York in 2005 in search of fragments from Jaxon's archives that might possibly have survived. He scoured antiquarian bookshops, flea markets and bazaars up and down Manhattan, thinking *something*, some scrap, might have escaped the trip to the landfill. He also plunged into the city archives looking for photographs of Honoré Jaxon's ammunition-case fort; and in all this, he came up with nothing. Jaxon had intended that the papers in his care would fill an Indigenous library in Saskatchewan. All traces had vanished. All traces of the millenarian daring of the Second Provisional Government, the all-gathering city on a hill in the North-West, were gone. How could beauty like that just disappear?

Poitras did discover in New York that Jaxon had been part of Coxey's Army, that march of unemployed workers on Washington in 1894, so his dreaming days had continued after Batoche and Chicago. Thus perhaps his fascination for Edward Poitras. Jaxon's lasting commitment to the metaphysical and political possibilities in Riel's visionary system clearly showed that the resistance was an animating ideal not just for Métis, but for a great many in the West, European settlers, as well as a number of original dwellers on the land.

◆

Edward Poitras, doing research for *New Breed* magazine in the 1980s, learned the source of the images that made up the Métis battle standard, the red hand and the wolf's head. The figures came from the biblical story of the tribe of Benjamin and the genocide attempted against it. Benjamin "is a wolf that raveneth" (Genesis 49:27). He was the child of Rachel, who died shortly after his birth. She had named him Benoni, "son of my sorrow," before death took her, but his father had renamed him Benjamin, "son of the right hand," that is, the preferred one, the one of good fortune. Judges 20 and 21 describes a later total war waged against the tribe of Benjamin, in which "the city, the people, all the animals and all that remained" (Judges 20:48) were destroyed. But a remnant survived in the wilderness.

CLOCKWISE FROM BOTTOM: Yvonne Chartrand, Krista Solheim and Marcus Merasty. Costumes by Robin Poitras. Set design by Edward Poitras. An NDH Rouge-gorge Collaboration by Edward Poitras and Robin Poitras. Photo: Daniel Paquet.

LEFT TO RIGHT: Marcus Merasty, Bill Coleman, Graham Kotowich, Eloi Homier. Costumes by Robin Poitras. Set design by Edward Poitras. An NDH Rouge-gorge Collaboration by Edward Poitras and Robin Poitras. Photo: Daniel Paquet.

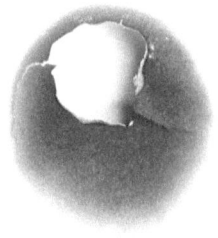

The House of Charlemagne

A DANCE IN THREE ACTS

Manitoba will become completely French-Canadian Métis. Five hundred years from now the Métis will number forty million souls. And in her turn she also will bear the joyous name of the "House of Charlemagne."
—LOUIS RIEL

ACT 1

NARRATOR

Mid-winter, rolling grey air over open water appearing through ice—chokecherry bluffs towering above the South Saskatchewan River grow dark by 4:00 p.m. Fruit on the branches stands frozen black. It's been snowing for a week. The rub of current along river ice is audible a quarter of a mile away. Four extrusions, small antlered craters, stir and bulk out of these valley humps, gathering form, male dancers, we eventually see, in long buffalo coats, which hang loosely on them, and rabbit fur hats, each with a single hand raised. They are costumed for the practice of science. Very slowly they begin to circle one another, humming deep in their chests, their heads tipped forward, chins pulled in, faces in half shadow. They continue to move even as the first begins to speak.

FIRST FIGURE *(crouched, within the circle, flinging looks side to side, lifting and falling on the balls of his feet)*

Si l'homme eût persévéré dans cet état de bonheur il s'y fut affectionné de plus en plus [de plus en plus, de plus en plus—*the phrase passed back and forth among the figures*]. Et plus il eût trouvé douce son intimité avec les essences actives [les essences actives, les essences actives], plus ils eût travaillé à la rendre parfaite. Son amour docile eût attiré à lui tous les jours une quantité nouvelle de monades actives [nouvelle de monades actives, nouvelle de monades actives]. Elles se fussent condensées dans sa personne à un degré considérable. Le poids de son corps eût fini par devenir comparativement léger dans le sein de leur densité.

The men move a half circle farther, facing away from one another. As they move, they repeat, in English, fragments of the speech, each taking a phrase in turn, in swaying voices—

If man had persevered in his state of happiness/ he would have become more and more loving./ Moreover he would have found sweet his intimacy with the active essences/ and furthermore he would have worked to render this intimacy perfect./ His kind or soft love would have attracted to him every day a fresh and new quantity of active monads./ These would have condensed in his person to a considerable degree./ The weight of his body would become comparatively/ lighter [lighter, *all whisper*] in the womb of their density, the thick weave of monadic organs and skin.

The dancers stop moving just before the Second Figure speaks.

SECOND FIGURE *(addressing the First Figure)*

So I often have heard you say: you stand by desire's cannon and fire it, and we, eros-sparks, soul quanta, no broader across the shoulders than blue moths, blunder in the flow of the shot.

Like so—*(he spins quickly a short way across the stage to the upper right, then turns and faces the First Figure)*

—and so we are *compressed*, *wedded*, in the blast, as in an electron accelerator, to the essences that are active and produce the choral hum harboured in things—there, you can hear it, listen, there, that grass stalk, that granite erratic, that bit of dry wood, that pelican footprint.

He shifts a few feet farther right, then turns to Louis Riel, the First Figure, lifting a stick to his ear.

There, hear it? You most of all, of course. Rustle of unbestilled quiddities, quaking, white water of their metabolism. This, as you have argued at length, as candles sank on many stands, in many holders, is the sound of the engine room of God's warm breath.

He dips and slides to his left.

It bends the grass as far as the eye can see.

His hand drifts to the horizon.

FOURTH FIGURE

We wish to be subtle.
We wish to grow eyes
and weightlessness
in the womb of objects.

SECOND FIGURE (*Honoré Jaxon*)

And, as you've said: "The prodigious concentration of the infinite essences in the loving man would have created for him the gift of subtle spirit. Cette concentration prodigieuse des essences infinies dans l'homme eût constitué pour lui le don de la subtilité." It's all there in that single sentence. The human individual in the world's birth canal.

Jaxon moves with great speed.

HONORÉ JAXON

Thus, swamped with explosive throw, soaked with battling light, we, pneuma packets, breath bearded, harden (concress, vanish, anneal, zig but do not zag) into ever-fleet dots *(he makes a gesture indicating the monadic shape)*, which Canadian grapeshot does not recognize and so misses.

Yes.

He shifts quickly four steps, then stops.

Their instruments lack this precision.

I have heard you on this, this spirito-physics. What you scratched with care on pieces of elk hide and paper scraps deep in Montana, far in winters, 1881 to 1884. Many pages of this philosophical-théologique synthesis now lost, blown away in snow or raised in random fires. Your voice sways in me. Canadian bullets do not recognize us. We swim in a band below their apparatus's range. Nor can the prime minister's lit cigars cruise forward, drop as arrow-fall to press red circles on the skin of our arms when we are in this clenched, robed state of the active essences.

LOUIS RIEL

Snider Enfield rifles snuff and break twigs near.

The four resume their circling, still looking at one another as rifle crackle is heard coming nearer. Wind stirs, snow circling their ankles. Occasionally they cast casual glances outward.

LOUIS RIEL

These coulees we move in wash our sleep

HONORÉ JAXON

yet appear perfectly motionless

LOUIS RIEL

but in fact are quick servants of the divinity above the sparks—they flowed from His breast when His heart was a four mile high ice sheet stretching from just below the Arctic Ocean near the Mackenzie River Delta to small yellow hills south of Lake Michigan.

The dancers move as if along the line of the glacial ice as it was 9,000 years ago when it began to melt, northwest to southeast.

We bend and weave ourselves to their supple course, seal motile tissue to hills' voluptuous, herd movement.

The dancers move as the coulees move, that is, toward the river.

LOUIS RIEL

Dakota hunger spoke as I knelt before it, put its lips to mine and breathed out. Silence four meters below the earth's surface there filled me, like a rifle barrel plugged with poured aluminum. From this hunger, placed in my throat, I received a will the size of a helium atom and had notched to my head an ear with the band-width of Western North America.

He pauses.

Look at how sweetly the river flows. There is nothing better than a river, the South Saskatchewan best of all, to shape a government's soulcraft.

A frozen smoke rises from the river. The men circle.

HONORÉ JAXON

I thought Plato and Christ
might do the trick, but this
is startling, clean. I completely believe you, every coal in me reddens
and flares. Mouths all through me, in molecules, ducts, make clear this
belief.

He spins, swirls away like a river eddy.

We are equally Pythagorean.

He smiles and moves.

I, somnambulant, on a significant cow path
from Prince Albert, routed through
the University of Toronto, drifted toward
a saltlick in Classics, you
from Red River Settlement
and St. Peter's Mission,
east and south of Fort Benton.

THIRD FIGURE

Numbers sing in the sky.

FOURTH FIGURE

Sing in the minerals in the earth.

LOUIS RIEL

Everything hums in algebraic concert.

FOURTH FIGURE

We are inebriated by the slender
shade in all things.

HONORÉ JAXON

Thus the state will be just and have moral beauty.
The gorgeous, unstoppable patterns shimmer
in what occupies the land, elk,
saskatoons, hills near Val Marie under their enflamed black sky,
like fire embers at the bottom of tunnels
or holes.
The patterns, transparencies, are laid
on latencies in our tongues and in our affections.

The four gather at the centre of the stage and look at a large map Riel has drawn from the folds of his robe and laid on the ground.

    FOURTH FIGURE *(tracing river systems on the map)*

Assiniboia, old Rupert's Land, re-architectured in your mouth, is the star map, perfect soul of all geometric forms, all decorous political, religious, economic shapes. Its light the spine. The place, as you say it, is a perfect city rising from your upturned face.

    THIRD FIGURE *(his finger just behind the tracing finger of the fourth man)*

I have seen myself, as this soul predicts,
music sing to mathematics,
and mathematics sing to philosophical chant, and this chant mouth
itself into the horse natures of rivers, the Athabasca,
Milk, Assiniboine, twin Saskatchewans and this
informs the movement of all heavenly bodies. All in
passion confluent. Everything speaks
in the ear of everything else.

    HONORÉ JAXON *(to Riel)*

And I know this and this
was confirmed for and in me when I entered
the ground with you and thought.
Lowered, blanketed, tied tight into
the hungry earth of your speech.
The olfactory current of bacteriaed, animaled soil actively
altered the course of my name. I am Honoré
now, Henry gone,
and, as Honoré, masticate light.

LOUIS RIEL

Pythagoreanism and philosophical
Taoism pool as icemelt
at the end of the long Upper Paleolithic
and this love makes the ground blow
songs and ratios into all of us
and we each have produced existence by this means;
it built us as bulbs in itself.
You and I are badger-mind,
wasp-intuition.
Let us say what you and I are
is (*laughing*) coyote-mentation. Thought as shape
in a glacier's gravel wash.
What the heavens say,
what leaf rot commands
and orchestrates in us, this thing
is our name, a shard of the One.
Thought's flower scent
is the politics that rises from our talk.
Utter Platonism, doubtless,
utter Platonism,
but one bouncing in a harness
suspended from horns in a running buffalo herd.

They hoist a flag, containing a wolf's head and red hand. A heavier array of gunshots are heard quite near.

HONORÉ JAXON

Middleton's battalions,
keeping their rectangularity, have made it nearly out
of the wild rose and saskatoon thickets
and approach the hill and church.
The heat of their guns brings on
an early summer.
Soon they will have a clear shot at pretty well all things.
Blue snowgeese migrate early.
You can hear sights
flick up on snipers' Sharps.

HONORÉ JAXON

My dragonfly eye
settles now on the Bulls
of Alexander VI.
Still time for research,
lectio divina, in these tipping days.
Through my vision's crepey wings
I feel the stipple of mountains and valleys
formed by consonants and vowels
on the curial page.
Alexander's saturnalian weight speaks, whistling
through meat lodged
in the papal teeth. He opens his mouth,
his conical tongue descends as a drill.
He views notional valleys and flats through moving palms
of lovers' limbs.
And he sees with strike-force flash the brand
beneath leaves, browsing moose, hundreds of miles
of burning forests
of the Spanish crown, as indigenous
to this place as
electron orbits.
Everything must receive the neck rope
clasping us to Christianity.
He instructs his will to advance by Latin's drumroll.
Let all be touched by the iron of the dark letters.

FOURTH FIGURE

The English, the Canadians,
coin-touching, onanistic,
lightly liquored Orangemen for once
believe and follow the pope.

THIRD FIGURE

They insert wear-white shims
and jimmy free certain names
in Alexander's decree
and tap in their own.
Then open their pockets to receive a pour of grain.

All move wildly, flakes in a blizzard.

LOUIS RIEL (*to Jaxon*)

All we did, from your U of T
fire tower, came,
enfin, from the unreasonable effectiveness
of mathematics in the natural
sciences.

He moves with delight, circling Jaxon.

Yet we are told
our world-thought was simply the tip
of the sight-cone streaming
from the mouldy eye of John Cabot.
For us, being seen by a European
who stood by full bags
on either side of his mare on the dock
could only be our creation.
Artillery creeping near
follows the calculations of their certainty.
The stormfront of their metaphysics
pillows before us. See the funneling cloud.

THIRD FIGURE

We had the alchemical equation
for gold here.

HONORÉ JAXON

There was a body
slipping among us, the rich
equation for love,
with its fine
wetblack nose.

ACT 2
Scene 1

Carts creak across the stage.

    PRISONER 1

The moon on this wagon's
sun-scraped planks is Pelidne Sulphur.
A butterfly so peculiar it is thought
mythical, hallucinated.

    PRISONER 2 *(in pain, holding his thigh)*

Uh—

    PRISONER 3

By the lemony bone
of its light …

    OTHERS *(like children)*

By the lemony bone of its
light …
By the lemony bone
of its light …

    PRISONER 3

… we receive raw blankets
and a gruelly food.

PRISONER 1

Tell me, could it be that none
of the books, those extraordinary, calm minds
so kind to us, beating,
yellow compound-eyed minds,
that circled us, stay
with us, alive? *Cloud of Unknowing, Mirror
of Simple Souls, and Those Who Remain Only
in Will and Desire* and suchlike—
were none of them saved?

PRISONER 2

None.
All the books burn.

The sky is enflamed with the burning library of Alexandria behind them, most of the last lost parts of the Massinahican *included in the conflagration.*

PRISONER 3

So we are orphaned.
The great cache of true cosmology
is muddled ash in Alexandria
teethflecks in the grey piles.
No light to love us. Pelidne Sulphur
is gone in a drift of ground mist.
No light remains that carries our smell.

PRISONER 1 *(gesturing to the guard)*

He has atomized our bone.

GUARD

Not so cheery,
I see, now that Britain holds
you in its square Roman heart.
You were Platonic fools we dismembered
to save you from the embarrassment your sky thought
would inevitably have brought you.
Thus the end of Sufism in Averroist Spain
and whatever was ticking over here.
Be grateful for the surgery

performed within the mess of your philosophical corruption.
The angelistic knife wielded.

PRISONER 3

Ooooh—Ooooh—

PRISONER 2

I tap my chest bone,
nothing taps back.

PRISONER 1

The lash has swept out
my breath.
What we have seen, I do believe, will
make a cloud, locust dark,
then settle again
as the Amritsar Massacre of 1919.

GUARD

We're nearly there.
You can see—look, there, as
the sun breaks—the crown
of the random gold pile
Edgar Dewdney arranged to mount
the east bank of Wascana Creek. A crow
lifts from its tip, a place, Dewdney believed, perfect
for toboggan parties, muskrat roasts,
warm in wealth's red-blond shade.
And there its conjoined
tower rises, all those bones—disarticulated
skeletons of bison, grizzly
bear, crocus, burrowing owl,
lady's slipper, SENĆOTEN, silver fox, Richardson's ground
squirrel, Michif, wheatgrass, blue, blue
grama grass, chipping sparrow, bluebirds, certain High Cree
nouns,
monarch butterflies, purple blazing star, anise swallowtails,
whooping cranes, meadowlarks, a million
snowgeese, Lakota syntax—awaiting
transliteration to phosphorous.
Now I uproot you from your chains.
I place, five miles before you,
a final cause so strong it could extract teeth,
it hauls you forward even as your bodies
gouge into the floor. I uproot you!
I uproot you! I uproot you!
Nature has been sucked into history.

The prisoners scream in protest.

GUARD

And I shove you toward the orange quake,
sour well burn on the horizon,
which will soak up what darkness you
carry and pull what is beneath its husk,
meager, impure, soon to be
unhappily disinterred light,
into its own perfect flesh.

The men, expelled from the carts, stumble forward through final sparse poplar groves, spiders like barrage balloons thickly above them. Two dancers are led off-stage by the guard into the gold mouth Dewdney and local authorities have erected at the edge of the settlement as a quarantine station. In the mouth, each inmate must pass through a deep central indentation, containing an emulsified version of Francis Bacon's Novum Organon, *as if it were a sheep-bath. So they learn the whole of the text by heart before they may walk forth and freely touch people.*

GUARD

Behold the book.
Take its liquids into your mouth
and eat what it thinks.
You have been selected for the state-
sponsored, strictly controlled experiment,
government science at its best. Can this
slag, this magnesium, copper hash, this lacustrine
hard yellow dirt be brought to wheat, and you
with it,
to participate, I mean, in wheat,
occluded light, minus shine
come to wheat's ingot,
absence of light to gold?
Best wishes and adieu.
Language by us has been weaponized.
I'll see you again, if at all, once we've been raised
to futures on the Winnipeg Grain Exchange.

Scene 2

Louis Riel and Honoré Jaxon are in separate cells in a larger enclosure, which is an immense cave, resembling Grotte de Chauvet, with many corridors feeding into it. They communicate telepathically.

    HONORÉ JAXON

Arctic blue butterflies fill this end of the pit,
this scooped, long dark, an ark, and leave
a pulse quivering like light from
sea ice on the cavern roof.
I smell cave bears and feel the wind
of their great movement.
It bends the light from my juniper-wick lamp above me—
the domed, ecclesiastical faces
of *Plebejus glandon* look back,
the wingspan of the beasts 28 millimeters
there in the shivering flame.
You feel the shadow of the bears
blown across you, as I've said; it persists—how their quick bodies
reshape the air.

    LOUIS RIEL *(he is speechless for five seconds, his mouth open, frozen)*

I am in a distance
mentioned in a book
(*The Cloud*)
and do not see
my body.
I do however see castles deep in the valleys
of this place, rain drops caught in trees,
a shimmering politics, a great dance
of various people and thousands
of bison.

HONORÉ JAXON

You can hear the books
still simmering in Alexandria.
They sound like grasshoppers feeding.
The guard is in a far part of the mansion
flicking lights on and off,
on contract with Sask Power.

He stirs about in his confined area.

A woman shifts gloom-pool
to deeper gloom
to shadow in one of the communicating tunnels,
gowned in wing movement. Golden eagle, blue heron.
Others report her, too: sometimes she is in a boat,
sometimes loose in air.
One of her arms is broken. She is the agent
intellect. Angel Gabriel, Holy Ghost.
Whoever she is she's left
her handprint in ochre outline on the wall.

LOUIS RIEL

I am my tongue,
which is Orpheus.
By my blue will
I will raise the gorgeous subterranean
long haired shade from dormition
                              under the earth, Valley Spirit,
and let her spread across the land,
a travelling grass flame.

ACT 3

Honoré Jaxon, in New York City, evicted from his basement apartment, is sitting on a rainy street, the nearly complete archives of the Last Provisional Government at Batoche stacked on the sidewalk around him. He wears a broad-brimmed buffalo hunter's hat and sits on one of the piles, his chin on his cane. People rush by him, returning from work, some with grocery bags. One of these, walking much more slowly than the rest, is the poet Hart Crane, alert Dionysian, a ghostly lion in rain-greyness, carrying a pocket full of loose oranges. He doesn't notice Jaxon, though he stops momentarily above him and raises his hands over his head as if in blessing, then joins them to light a cigarette, leaves.

    HONORÉ JAXON (*he makes to speak but cannot, his mouth locked*)

The government we made dwelt in the air.
The river, frozen or open, beamed its *li*
into the bottom of its skeleton.
Poplar. Stone lichen.
Riel sang it up there and it grew
to be
eatable illumination.

The wind picks up. Some of the papers scatter.

HONORÉ JAXON

Nine years after the Little Bighorn
we tried it and talked
a bright polis into lifting its
gleaming payload.
Poplar. Métis and white farmers,
circling Cree.
We called through cannon smoke
to one another.

More wind. Rain.

They are all dead.
I see them as painted logs
laid out in lines four feet
below the ground. A plough wind
could raise them. Or news
of a large herd spy-glassed west
of Williston or Willow Bunch. Operatic
disgust could get them up and out,
missiling from the ground.

Sounds of sirens, beeping, backing up trucks. He sits at the foot of the Empire State Building. Winds howl between buildings.

HONORÉ JAXON

I try to keep the swimming
papers calm and hobbled
with my hands. I have become their
sole living relative. And they need
me as their shepherd, signing authority, personal
trainer, priest and source
of their food,
but they bob and flash in elliptical
deliria. Holding still, you will note,
Kepler's geometry.
Their punctuation shakes
out of them—leaf fall.

He circles the stacks of papers, trying to catch the sailing sheets.

How strange that out of
all that beauty
nothing but an old
unfixed-by-address man in a large hat
and blowing papers (which
hold the equations
for building a machine
called the *Massinahican*,
which disgorges food
and beauty endlessly, stackable
beauty) remains.
Riel's *Massinahican*, toucan-
and flicker-feather blanketed.
How strange this is the result

of such thousand horsepowered longing.
I hear the circling
brown herd below the earth.
I hear the talk there
among numerous hunched others.
The kingdom of heaven—vast, superb,
thrilled, shivering,
a settlement that would take weeks
to cross on foot,
gigantic ship-like contraption,
bigger than Hubble, much bigger, equal
in fact to what it views—
indeed came near, aimless,
engineless, drifting at ear height
and grazed our skulls.
The perfume, wooze and wobble,
of our consequent concussion persists,

vulnus amoris, and clings to everything
like heat lines in air
and it trembles through the ground
in faint aftershock.
The talk goes on.
It goes on. It goes on.
It goes on.
It shivers up our
bodies' stalks.

NOTES AND ACKNOWLEDGEMENTS

Quotations from Louis Riel's works in Part I, *Massinahican*, are drawn from the following sources:

p. 13: *Système philosophico-théologique* [Montana, 1881–4] in *The Collected Writings of Louis Riel*, Volume II, ed. Gilles Martel, University of Alberta Press, 1985, 387.

p. 14: *Système philosophico-théologique* [Montana, 1881–4] in *The Collected Writings of Louis Riel*, Volume II, ed. Gilles Martel, University of Alberta Press, 1985, 388.

p. 18: Prière à la Vierge Marie, in *The Collected Writings of Louis Riel*, Volume II, ed. Gilles Martel, University of Alberta Press, 1985, 340.

p. 19: Lettre à Joseph Riel, in *The Collected Writings of Louis Riel*, Volume II, ed. Gilles Martel, University of Alberta Press, 1985, 328.

p. 20: "La religion ...": *Système philosophico-théologique* [Montana, 1881–4] in *The Collected Writings of Louis Riel*, Volume II, ed. Gilles Martel, University of Alberta Press, 1985, 394.

p. 20: "Le sexe est dans ...": *Système philosophico-théologique* [Montana, 1881–4] in *The Collected Writings of Louis Riel*, Volume II, ed. Gilles Martel, University of Alberta Press, 1985, 399.

The quotations from Louis Riel's works in Part II, *The House of Charlemagne*, are drawn from the following sources:

p. 33: *Système philosophico-théologique* [Montana, 1881–4] in *The Collected Writings of Louis Riel*, Volume II, ed. Gilles Martel, University of Alberta Press, 1985, 387.

p. 36: *Système philosophico-théologique* [Montana, 1881–4] in *The Collected Writings of Louis Riel*, Volume II, ed. Gilles Martel, University of Alberta Press, 1985, 387.

The quotation from Honoré Jaxon's letter on p. 14 is from *Honoré Jaxon: Prairie Visionary* by Donald B. Smith, Regina: Coteau Books, 2007, 62.

The epigraph on p. 31 is from *The Diaries of Louis Riel*, ed. Thomas Flanagan, Edmonton: Hurtig Publishers, 1976, 166.

I wish to thank Edward Poitras, Robin Poitras, and New Dance Horizons for their invitation to me to participate in the production of *The House*. I wish also to thank Jan Zwicky for her editorial eye and Mia Anderson for her help with the French translations. I thank as well the University of Chicago Press for permission to quote from Peter Balakian's *Ziggurat*.

ᑭᓄᑲ

OSKANA POETRY & POETICS
BOOK SERIES

Publishing new and established authors, Oskana Poetry & Poetics offers both contemporary poetry at its best and probing discussions of poetry's cultural role.

Jan Zwicky—*Series Editor*

Advisory Board
Roo Borson
Robert Bringhurst
Laurie D. Graham
Louise Bernice Halfe
Tim Lilburn
Randy Lundy
Daniel David Moses
Duane Niatum
Gary Snyder

For more information about publishing in the series, please see:
www.uofrpress.ca/poetry

PREVIOUS BOOKS IN THE OSKANA POETRY & POETICS BOOK SERIES:

Measures of Astonishment: Poets on Poetry, presented by the League of Canadian Poets (2016)

The Long Walk, by Jan Zwicky (2016)

Cloud Physics, by Karen Enns (2017)

www.ingramcontent.com/pod-product-compliance
Lightning Source LLC
Chambersburg PA
CBHW020627300426
44112CB00010B/1226